I0617531

POEMS AS A KEY TO LIFE

GWINT L. FISHER

GHOSTWRITERS & ETC., LLC

Copyright © 1992 Gwint L Fisher
All rights reserved.

No part of this book may be reproduced in any form or by any electronic or mechanical means, including information storage and retrieval systems, without written permission from the author, except for the use of brief quotations in a book review.

GhostWriters & Etc., LLC
PO Box1062
Long Beach, WA 98631
www.poemsasakeytolife.com

1-(360)-232-4990

ISBN: 979-8-9894674-4-0: e-book
ISBN: 979-8-9894674-0-2: Paperback
Library of Congress Control Number: 2023923310

Any people depicted in stock imagery provided by Pixabay Images are models, and such images are being used for illustrative purposes only.

Certain stock imagery © Pixabay Images.
Print information available on the last page.

CONTENTS

ABOUT THIS BOOK

This book of poetry contains over 30 poems which were written over 30 years ago and recently Published. The majority are written in traditional rhythmic form, whereas others are written in contemporary abstract form. These poems were written during times of transition involving life, love, and loss. If you believe in love, and if you have ever lost that special someone for some unknown or known reason, this is the book for you. If you have ever had to make life changing decisions that affected you emotionally, then this book is a must read. Remember that "Poetry is The Key to Life", enjoy.

LUST? OR LOVE?

Was it lust when we met? Or was it really love at first sight?

The thrill I received once our conversation became just a little more than intimate, was this Lust? Or Love?

The feeling of that warm sensation that ran through my body, was it Lust? Or Love?

The excitement I got at the thought of one of your passionate kisses, was that Lust? Or Love?

To think of a future together as boyfriend and girlfriend then husband and wife, is that Lust? Or Love?

To want you to have my children and raise them to be as beautiful as you are, is that Lust? Or Love?

Who can really distinguish the thin line between Lust? Or Love?

Whether the thought be of holding you, kissing you, speaking to you, or even having my children, one question is for sure, am I Lusting? Or Loving?

Gwint L. Fisher

"ONE DAY"

One day you will see how much you really mean to me.

One day you will know that my love is true to only you.

One day your eyes will open and maybe you'll say, "my God how could I have let love like that slip away?"

One day you will realize that the truth hurts, but you'll be big enough to except it and grow.

One day your life will be prosperous with Love, Happiness, and Understanding.

One day you will learn that things you have said and done has brought hurt.

One day you will love like I have, and one day you will hurt like I do.

One day you will know pain and sorrow, and the way it falls hard upon you. But until that day may God always watch over and bless you true!

Gwint L. Fisher

"IF I ONLY HAD A HEART TO GIVE"
(ODE, TO MY LUSTING WAYS)

If I only had a heart to give, oh to you I'd give this heart.

I would give it along with all my love to enjoy for now, and many days to come.

To you I'd give this heart so true, to fulfill your life with things a new, romantic encounters, elegant dinners, roses and carnations whose beau-tiful aroma would remind me of you.

All these things plus many more I'd give so willingly just so you may enjoy? But to give you this heart would be a lie, for someone else enjoys, with me this heart of mine.

She's just as pretty and lovely too, she's a woman who's intelligence shines through and through.

Her smile is wonderfully bright, Her hugs are lovingly tight, and Her touch, O well what can I say, seems to thrill me each and every day.

You see this heart I'd like to give belongs to someone with whom I live. Her perfumes that I smell, Her dinners that I've eaten are always roman-tic, and can't be beaten.

If I could give this heart to thee, it would only be for "Lust" you'd see. Only to be given for a short, short time to gain your trust and manipulate your mind.

For what you would get, would not be pure, for the heart I speak of is safe and well secure!

Gwint L. Fisher

"FROM THESE LIPS COMES A KISS"

Sometimes warm, sometimes wet, sometimes passionate, and yet the best you never forget.

Most are caring, most are loving, most are sensual and always combined with a lot of hugging.

From these lips comes a kiss full of warmth, understanding, and just a hint of delicate sweetness.

There's lots of tenderness, there's lots of compassion, there's lots of intimacy, and all of these are in well-mannered fashion.

From these lips, a kiss you'd receive, never to forget that thrilling moment of ecstasy.

From these lips, a kiss you'd receive, never to forget the past, and enjoy the present, I'm more then sure you'd start planning our future as parents.

For you see one thing that I really know as our life together would continue to grow, is that from these lips would come, a lovingly warm, romantic, and sensuous Kiss.

Gwint L. Fisher

"Smack"

MY LADY IN RED

You've really got to see how beautiful she looks to me, wearing the dress that's red, and fits beyond belief.

She's extremely extraordinary, the way she walks, the grace she uses, and the way the wind blows through her soft silky hair.

Truly, it's unbelievable the red dress she wears. It looks so tight, but fits just right, and hugs each curve from her neck to her derriere.

My Lady in Red is not only beautiful through and through, she's also cunning, intelligent, and has enough common sense for both me and you.

She's so exciting to watch, and thrilling to see, she's glamorous from the distant, and up close- wooooo weeeee!

That red dress she wears is more than pretty, it brings out a mystique and accentuates her beauty.

I just have to say it is not only red that makes her look this way, for my lady is just as exciting in black, blue, or even an amethyst color such as purple too.

So when you see my Lady In Red, I'm sure that you'll agree; she's not only beautiful to you, but most of all her beauty's just for me!

Gwint L. Fisher

"FORGIVE ME PLEASE?"

Forgive me please for the things I've done, that bought this pain to you.

I'm sorry for telling all those lies, but it seem the right thing to do.

Oh forgive me please for making you cry in such a sad, sad, way.

But it slipped my mind, at that time, that you really loved me too.

For I didn't know how far it would go when we argued like fools, but when you said- "That's it, it's dead, just take your clothes we're through!"

My mind seemed to pause, my body seem to stall, I wondered- "My God what will I do?"

Oh forgive me please I'm on my knees begging, praying, and just saying- "How much I want only you!"

All I ask this one last time, is to look at me, hold my hands and maybe you'll see, that you're my Hearts Desire.

I ask Somehow, someway, if it's in your Heart, just look at me, I'm trying to say "Oh Forgive Me Please, Please, Please This Day?"

Gwint L. Fisher

BEAU – TI – FUL

I can say, so it seems, that beauty of all colors have I seen. Beauty that's Unique, and that has Style, and Grace, Beauty that can stop men right in their place.

I've been witness to Gorgeous, Exotic, and Delicious Beauty in front of me, of which only God could have Created to See.

Beauty of Culture, Ethnic, and Social Grace has always intrigued me with a Mystical Taste.

Beauty from within will never Stall, from the Heart, through the Mind, and to the Spirt. Beauty such as this can be found by One and All.

But, of course the Beauty that's most Beautiful to see, is that which is seen through the "Eyes of the Beholdee."

Gwint L. Fisher

<u>LONELINESS!</u>

Loneliness to Thee, is a selfish thing for me.

Loneliness can be a sad, sad time for some of Thee.

To be alone in this mans World, is like being stuck in some far off Jail.

To be alone, and this you'll see, is surely no fun for either you or me.

That feeling of loneliness can run deep in your vein, to make you Feel self-pity and shame.

That feeling of loneliness can Creep on you, so please my friend watch what you do.

So when it seems that no one's there, and you're feeling all alone.

Just remember, there is someone, who's waiting for you to come Home.

Gwint L. Fisher

"WHERE WE'VE MET BEFORE?"

When I saw your face, I tried to figure the place where we've met before.

I've tried my memory's Video Tapes, and I only come up blank. I've searched and wondered through my mind, but still, I can't find a thing. Where have we met before? Was it at a Theater Show? Or perhaps a Concert or Two? Maybe at the Beach where the Sun Shined Bright on You?

What I do know , is that you look real Nice to Me, someone who I'd like to full fill all my Fantasies.

So maybe in this "Life" I'll remember for ever more, Who You are, What You're all about, and most of all "Where We've Met Before!"

Gwint L. Fisher

"TIME IS SOMETHING!!"

Time is something that's Precious and Sweet. Always reminding us that God's Unique.

Either moving fast or moving slow time is something that always Goes.

Time is something that should be met, no matter where or how far, it must be Kept.

Sometimes early, sometimes late, time is something that to you it will Make or Break.

If time, you think, is on your side; then let me tell you "Don't Believe that Lie."

For there's only one who can tell you True, that time's on Him, and Never You!

Gwint L. Fisher

"YOUR EYES, YOUR SMILE"

When we met, I was caught, by your Eyes, your Smile.

They seem to me, so Bright, so Free, they showed your Elegance in Style.

It was as if I were showered by sunshine, then bathed in Ultraviolet Rays. Your Eyes your Smile, are like the rising of the Sun, letting the world know that another day has just begun.

A day that's so clear with white soft puffy clouds and a wondrous Blue Sky. To me your Eyes, and your Smile are the "Bright Points" in my life.

Ever reminding me of the "Love and Romance" that you can bring into our Lives.

Gwint L. Fisher

26

"ONCE AGAIN!"

Once again, I find myself caught between my Heart and Mind, just trying to figure-out weather it's going to be right this Time.

I've fallen for someone who fills my heart with Love and Joy.

So it seems this time I'll be treated right, and not played with like a Toy.

Once again, I've found a Friend and a Lover too. I'm on my way, I'm feeling great just thinking good things of You.

My Heart is constantly telling me that this is the one for you, but my Mind continues to say, "to trust her you're the Fool!"

Once again, I'm the one who's Emotions will be disrupted. I'll feel real bad, oh so sad, and most of all Disgusted.

But in the End, once again, I'll bounce back Strong, and Sure, because in the End, Once Again, "My Love Has Found No Cure!!!"

Gwint L. Fisher

28

"MY LOVE"

My Love is like a Mountain Stream, Beautiful to look at, Cool and Sweet to the taste, and Cleansing to the touch.

My Love can flow through and around all Obstacles to make it to its appointed Destinations, your Heart and Soul.

My Love seems to gather no Moss or Foreign Debris, but always Sustains Life and Branches in all Directions.

My Love is sometimes hard to reach and can be a very winding type of Love. My Love, once under control, flows and follows a straight path to a pool of ever awaiting Romance, Kindness, Joy, Happiness, and ever lasting Ecstasy.

"That's how Far and Deep My Love Flows!"

Gwint L. Fisher

30

"I LOVE YOU; BUT I REALLY DON'T!!"

I Love You for the Pain and Sorrow that you've given me; But I Really Don't!

I Love You for that time you Cheated on Me too; But I Really Don't

I also Love You for all those times that we Argued like "Fools";

But I Really Don't!

I Love You for all those "Lies" that you said were true; But I Really Don't!

I Love You for the times you had me Worried and Frighten

When you stayed out all night; But I Really Don't!

I'm just trying to say, that this isn't the Way, I really wanted to Love You, Each and Every Day!

I say, "I Love You", so please don't even try, to find out the Reason Why; "Because I Really Don't!!!"

Gwint L. Fisher

"THE WAIT"

Long lines, long waits are just a Mental Torture, society has them there only for Certain Cultures.

Patients is a Virtue, so I'm told, but to believe that sometimes my mind must be Cold!

But as I stand or sit through that long, long, wait, I seem to notice others who have Fallen upon such ill Fate.

Some are sad, some are angry, and some are truly Worried. Like myself they're only hoping that this will surely Hurry.

The only wait that is really long and filled with fear and Horror are courts, Doctors, and Social Services in a mad, mad Flurry.

But the wait that is really worth those Theater, or Concert ticket wait, the one that's worth being patient for? Is that Doctor saying "Sir, tis a Healthy, Beautiful, baby your Wife has just Bore!"

Gwint L. Fisher

????

I've really got to know, how far must I go, to find my Hearts Desire?

Must I Fly, Should I Drive, or can I walk to Fined Her?

Please Oh Please tell me now, that You're the one who set "My Heart A Fire?"

Gwint L. Fisher

IF LOVE WERE!

If Love were honey, it would taste as Sweet as You.

If Love were a Rose, it would smell as Beautiful as You.

If I were Love and Love were lost, I'd only want to be Found by You.

If Love were time, and as time goes, so would our Love for as long as, who Knows?

If I were Love and as Love is True, I'd only want to be Loved By You.

So as Time goes, and Honey tastes, as a Rose smells, this must I say, may no one ever take Your Place!

Gwint L. Fisher

"IF WE COULD LOVE!"

If we could Love, I'd Love only You.

If we could Love, I'd be True to You.

If we could Love, I'd share all my Dreams with You

If we could Love, I'd take you now, to Hug and Kiss and say, "OH WOW!"

If we could Love, We'd fly away too far off places so We could Play.

If we could Love, I'd like to say, my Love for You Would always Stay.

But as it Stands upon this day, "Is it only me who could Love this Way?"

Gwint L. Fisher

BLUE COMPARED TO YOU!

The red means Love, The White means Sincerity, and The Yellow means Friends. The Blue is one that's Special to the End!

It reminds me that love is truly unique. The Blue is truly full of Mystique.

It can only be found in a Secret and Magical place. The Blue is Wonderous and takes not Second Place.

It's Beauty you'll see is glamorous with Glee.

The Blue to me is very Special and Sweet.

It smells like no other Fascinating and Strange.

The Blue has a smell that will never leave nor Change.

It can only be compared to one thing this is true.

The Blue reminds me of the "Romantic Love" I Have for You!

Gwint L. Fisher

42

TWENTY-FOUR AND NO MORE

Twenty-four hours is what I've ask of you, just to show I'm really True.

Twenty-four hours is all I need, to bring you happiness and a little Glee.

Twenty-four hours of your time, to show how much I'd like you to be Mine.

Twenty-four hours from head to toe, to show you how far my Kisses would Go.

Twenty-four hours of fun and games to wine and dine and show you no Shame.

Twenty-four hours is what I've ask of Thee.

Twenty-four hours "Just forMe."

Gwint L. Fisher

44

MY LOVER OR MY FRIEND?

What will it be for Thee?

Will we Hug and Kiss or will we just Sit and Wish?

Will we walk and hold Hands, or will we just make Plans?

Will we enjoy one another One on One, or will we be hoping that we have some Fun?

Will we enjoy Gazing into each other's Eyes, knowing our Love will never Die?

Or will we sit and wonder Why we never met Eye to Eye?

Will we call and talk for Hours or just drop a line and say "How are Ya?"

Will you be my Lover please? So I can Cherish all of Thee, from now until Eternity!

But if it's Friends that must we be, this to shall be fine with me.

The Question is: "What will it be; My Lover or My Friend for Eternity?"

Gwint L. Fisher

46

"DREAMS AND WISHES"

When I dream, I dream of You!
My dreams are long and sometimes Strange. But it seems I always awake to the call of your Name.

When I wish, I wish for You!
My wishes are like all others this is True, Outrageous, Outlandish, and always Misconstrued.

When I dream, Weather they be Good dreams or Bad dreams!
My dreams can be of Holding and Loving you True, but they can also be of Arguing with you Too.

When I wish, Weather they be Good wishes, or Bad wishes!
My wishes are always of Money and reaching for the Stars, but in Gods eyes I have gone just too Far.

But of Dreams and Wishes it must be Construed, that most definitely some of them do come True.
And that in Reality we call it Deja'vu!

Gwint L. Fisher

"IT WILL NEVER BE THE SAME"

No matter how hard I try to forget the past, it will always be there. How can it be? Who says it won't? But what if I really tried? The answers to these questions still linger heavy in my mind; it can never, nor ever be the same.

The things we did, the places we went, the love we truly shared. Those intimate conversations, the romantic evenings, and of course the prayers together we prayed.

All these things can never, nor ever really happen again. You see the pain I've endured, and most of all the heart that's been broken and mended over again just lets me know that a life together would never nor ever be the same.

The uneasiness, the lack of trust, and those constant worrying feelings would all seem to filter up; and boy would I feel disgust!

You see we can never love again unless it's in sin. And with the way God watches, what's life with only lust and no romance!

I guess the Love we had then, will remain in the past. To look back upon, learn from, and not continue to ask, "how can it be?" Who says it won't? But what if I really tried? These are all questions that will never be answered because they will never be asked. You see I already know there can be no future with my "Past."

Gwint L. Fisher

"SURE, I HAVE A SMILE"

Sure, I have a smile just for you, I have a smile that's more than true.

Sure, I have a smile that's bright, and loving that I'd like to share with you.

You see I have a smile that lets you know that life is wonderful, no matter what happens or where you go.

Sure, I have a smile that I would like to give, to the Homeless, the Poor, and most of all to those Sick and Dying Kids.

For my smile carries laughter and sounds of joy. My smile has strength and shows great poise.

Sure, I have a smile just for you and I hope you have one that you can share with me too?

Gwint L. Fisher

"GOODBYE!!"

These two words are the hardest words I've ever had to say – "GOODBYE!"

You see I can no longer hold on and wait for you to decide – "GOODBYE!"

As I fight through this pain, my attitude has began to change and I really must say – "GOODBYE!"

I now see there's nothing I can say or do to keep you as a part of my life –"GOODBYE!"

The hurt I'll go through and the torture I must endure when I see your face, knowing you'll never be mine – "GOODBYE!"

But this I can say, the lessons have been learned, the pain has and will be endured, most of all the growth will always continue – "GOODBYE!"

So, to you my Love, I leave you with the saddest word I know – "GOODBYE!"

Gwint L. Fisher

"I THINK I WILL, I WILL!"

I think I will, I will, I think? Because when
I think I will, I will. To think and will means you
will, because thinking I will surely means I will.
But sometimes I find I will, think that is, due to the
fact that I will think, and when I think I will Oh God,
what a will. While thinking and willing sometimes I
find myself feeling and oh boy I surely don't want to
think that will. So for now I'll continue to think and I
will, and while I'm thinking and willing, I pray that
there's no feeling especially while I'm willing and
thinking. So in closing I will say, remember to think
before you will because while you're thinking I'll be
willing and thinking. That I think I will. But when
I think I will, I know I've thought too much.

Gwint L. Fisher

"CAUGHT BETWEEN TWO LOVES"

It has been some time, since I've found myself, caught between two loves.

Wondering and Feeling the same emotion, so it seems, for two, trying to figure out which one is really true.

Caught between two loves is where I've been before, trying to see which one will be exciting and not a total bore.

When caught between two loves I weigh the pros and cons, I try to find the good points but most of all the bad ones.

I'm caught between two loves with whom each I feel the same. Their smiles are nice, their conversations are bright, and with these I feel no shame.

A decision must be made, on who I'll make no trade. It must be right, they're both real nice. But it can only be one for me and not two, because my life is not the same.

Gwint L. Fisher

"ONE LAST KISS"

That one last kiss still lingers in my mind, the time, the place, and even those last few lines.

It's a kiss I will never ever forget, for it was our very, very last Kiss!

You see it was a Kiss to say Goodbye, a Kiss to say so long, a Kiss to say "Farewell, my Love I must be moving on."

For some, one last Kiss can be cold and cruel, it can mean the end of a relationship where the two only dueled.

But for others that one last kiss came from the understanding, that their relationship has become just too Demanding.

There are no new places to go, no new things to do, they can find no more Excitement or Fun for Two.

So, in parting my love this is all I can say, "Just one Last Kiss", and I'll be out of your life and on my Way.

Gwint L. Fisher

60

"PAIN AND SUFFERING"

Pain can be suffered through many ways, to describe them all could take days.\

But the pain I've encountered in this lifetime, has brought hurt and sorrow which are serious feelings of the mind.

So, for you here are a few that bring these feelings of being sad and blue.

Pain and Suffering is when your true love no longer loves you.

Pain and Suffering is knowing that, that person will never come back into your life. But you continue to hold onto the love you have for them.

Pain and Suffering is when someone very close to you has died and gone to that resting place in the sky.

Pain and Suffering is when you realize the child you've raised is no longer a child anymore.

But to know Pain and have Suffered through it, is truly a major job to complete.

To Suffer through Pain and endure the hardship is truly a major growth in life, to which we must thank our lord "Jesus Christ."

Gwint L. Fisher

"THE FRIENDSHIP OF TRUE FRIENDS"

To be my friend doesn't take a lot, It's having the willingness to share your friendship; rather than not.

Being my friend means having the honesty in one's self, to be able to let me know when I really need your help.

The friendship I gather from my friends gives me strength! It makes me wonder do I really have that many complaints? These friends of mine, this I can say, are friends who will come through in the worst of times.

Not once, nor twice, my friends' friendship goes beyond the normalcy of just being nice.

Finding friends like these you might think take years, decades or possibly even centuries. But really all I know, is that friends, like these have been right under my nose. All I've ever had to do is pick up that thing called a telephone.

Gwint L. Fisher

"WHAT IS NORMAL FOR ME?"

For me I will never know what it's like to be normal, for I have gone past the ideal of normalcy. On a day-to-day basis I pick up my script, to act out my part of being a normal person – "Yea that's it."

I deal with anger and I deal with stress, I'm reminded each day I'm not normal and for me that's not hard to forget.

Like most people, who lead normal lives, each day is taken oh so for granted. Their life seems to flow so free, straight, and narrow without the vagueness of being slanted.

My dreams of being a normal person are now far and few, they no longer exist for me but perhaps they do for you.

Each day for me is now filled with a prayer, a friend, and a meeting of the minds, all of which seemingly takes away all these past painful good, and bad times. Δ

Gwint L. Fisher

"TO THEE WITH WHOM I RARELY SEE!"

To thee my child I send to you my thoughts of Love and Joy, to thee I send these thoughts instead of little Tinker Toys.

I write these words just to say I Love you each and every day!
I know it's hard oh my child to believe these words I say, but my intentions are good, my heart is true, and my undying Love is always there for you.

To thee with whom I rarely see, I send these thoughts of mine; to hope and pray that on someday, we'll have a really good time.

It's just as hard for me my child not to be close to you, but you've got to know I miss you so, and I hope I'll see you soon.

So please my child be strong and grow, for soon we'll be together, talking, laughing, having fun, and getting to know each other "A Whole Lot Better".

Love Always
Gwint L. Fisher

ABOUT THE AUTHOR

The Author is merely a man who went through an emotional time while recovering from Substance Abuse and wanted to express his heart felt Love of Life in poetry form. He truly believes that most people in and out of recovery will appreciate the sincerity in these poems and come to love them. He has no degree in writing or creative arts, only a few courses in creative writing and poetry while in college.

BIBLIOGRAPHY

Pixabay.com/illustrations/marilyn-monroe-female-lips-6209936

Pixabay.com/illustrations/ai-generated-hourglass-sand glass7914871

Pixabay.com/photos/rose-flower-dew-dewdrops-droplets165819

Pixabay.com/photos/flower-blue-rose-fantasy-dream-4252326

Pixabay.com/photos/kiss-festive-lipstick-red-bold-562556

Pixabay.com/illustrations/hourglass-glass-isolated-time 4738338

Pixabay.com/illustrations/blow-kiss-moon-heart-night-sky-5864823